Great Big Giggles & Jokes

Compiled by Anna Pansini
Illustrated by Carolyn Loh

Troll Associates

Library of Congress Cataloging-in-Publication Data

Pansini, Anna.
  Great riddles, giggles & jokes / compiled by Anna Pansini;
illustrated by Carolyn Loh.
    p.   cm.
  Summary: A collection of jokes and riddles submitted by elementary
school students from around the United States.
    ISBN 0-8167-1915-2 (lib. bdg.)   ISBN 0-8167-1916-0 (pbk.)
    1. Riddles, Juvenile.   2. Wit and humor, Juvenile.   [1. Riddles.
2. Jokes.]   I. Loh, Carolyn, ill.   II. Title.
PN6371.5.P36   1990
818'.54020809282—dc20
                                                    89-5200

A TROLL BOOK, published by Troll Associates,
Mahwah, NJ 07430

What's Your Favorite Joke?

That's the question we asked kids across America as part of our **Great Giggle & Riddle Contest.** And the mail came pouring in! Riddles, knock-knock jokes, funny lines about animals, school, and ghosts—we received thousands of great jokes from kids.

You'll find the very best of the bunch compiled into two books—this one, and a companion book called *Best Jokes & Riddles*. Each book is filled with 350 jokes that will make you smile, giggle, or laugh out loud.

We've included the contestant's name with each joke. (When we received duplicate jokes, we chose the earliest entry.) Both books contain an alphabetical listing of winners, along with their age or grade, school, and school address.

Finally, a very special thanks to all the children who entered the contest, and the teachers who encouraged them.

Monster Madness

In what month was King Kong born?
Ape-ril.

Heather Busser

Why did Godzilla eat Tokyo instead of Rome?
Because spicy Italian food always gives him indigestion.

Michael Pedersen

First Monster: You don't have a brain in your head.
Second Monster: Which head?

Matthew Grande

How can you tell if a monster likes you?
He'll take another bite.

Wesley Petersen

Why did Frankenstein squeeze his girlfriend?
Because he had a crush on her.

Mike Komisin

What did the monster eat after the dentist pulled his tooth?
The dentist.

Tawnya Williams

How does a monster count to 101?
On his fingers and toes.

Chris Lomax

What is a two-headed monster's favorite ball game?
A double-header.

John Stoeckle

Why did the giant get lost?
Because his head was always in the clouds.

Natasha Boothe

Strange Monster: Madam, your son is smelly, dirty, gruesome and hasn't any manners!
Mother Monster: Thank the man for the nice compliment, Junior.
Jason St. Jean & Kevin Collins

What happened when the monster ate the electric company?
He was in shock for a week.

John Mullins

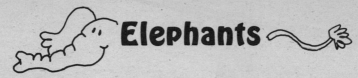

Elephants

How do you get down from an elephant?
You don't. You get down from a duck.

Kathryn Margaret Evans

Why did the elephant paint himself all different colors?
So he could hide in the crayon box.

Susan Allene Clark

Why do elephants have wrinkles?
Because they're so hard to iron.

Okwuoma Ohia

Why did the elephant put skates on before he went to bed?
Because he wanted to get rolling in the morning.

Jennifer Thomas

Why can't an elephant ride a tricycle?
Because it doesn't have a thumb to ring the bell.

Brent Thomas

First Person: How do you shoot a blue elephant?
Second Person: With a blue elephant gun.
First Person: Right. How do you shoot a pink elephant?
Second Person: With a pink elephant gun?
First Person: No. You hold its nose until it turns blue, then you
   shoot it with a blue elephant gun.

Krystal Coles

Why do elephants wear sunglasses?
So no one will recognize them.

Katina Fairley

**Why are elephants such poor
dancers?**
Because they have two left feet.

Denise Ramon

**What time is it when an elephant
sits on a fence?**
Time to get a new fence.

Jessica Groce

Why can't elephants go swimming at the beach?
Because they can't keep their trunks up.

Eileen Boulden

5

Riddles

What goes "oom oom"?
A cow walking backwards.

Krystal Fornoff

What's black, white, black, white, black, white, and green?
Three skunks fighting over a pickle.

Noah Miller

What coat is only put on when it is wet?
A coat of paint.

Jennifer Durre

What starts with E and ends with E and has one letter in it?
An envelope.

Jennifer Engelbrecht

Who built the first underground tunnel?
A worm.

Linda Petrecca

What does the Great Wall of China have that the Chinese didn't put there?
Cracks.

Scott Cearfoss

When will a net hold water?
When the water turns to ice.

Sarah Posegate

What do you lose every time you stand up?
Your lap.

Shannon Wittkopp

How can you take one away from nine and get ten?
Use Roman numerals. $IX - I = X$.

Carrie Burns

The more you take away, the bigger it gets. What is it?
A hole.

Juanette Schrier

Riddles

What is the difference between the earth and the sea?
One is dirt-y and the other is tide-y.

Aaron Jackson

Why weren't dinosaurs allowed to drive cars?
Because there were too many Tyrannosaurus wrecks.

Brian McKenzie

How many letters are in the alphabet?
Eleven. T-h-e a-l-p-h-a-b-e-t.

LaTosha Manbeck

What is often brought to the table, cut, yet never eaten?
A deck of cards.

Jackie Lewis

What has five eyes and a mouth?
The Mississippi River.

Carol Lee Smith

A man rode to Texas on Thursday, stayed for three days, and came back on Thursday. How can this be?
His horse's name is Thursday.

Lydell Thomas

What has 4 legs, 4 wheels, a long neck and spots?
A giraffe on a skateboard.

Shannon Fitzgerald

What are the four seasons?
Salt, pepper, vinegar and mustard.

Tommy Murphy

What is gray, has four legs, and a trunk?
A mouse going on vacation.

James Russell

What has ears but can't hear?
Corn.

Robyn Van Dyke

7

Knock-Knocks

Knock! Knock!
Who's there?
Rita.
Rita who?
Rita book, you might learn something.

Tom Gould

Knock! Knock!
Who's there?
Police.
Police who?
Police open the door, I'm tired of knocking.

Melissa Radford

Knock! Knock!
Who's there?
Henrietta.
Henrietta who?
Henrietta worm that was in his apple.

Yvonne Moyet

Knock! Knock!
Who's there?
Ice cream.
Ice cream who?
Ice cream 'cause I'm a cheerleader.

Jessica Rosario

Knock! Knock!
Who's there?
Carrie.
Carrie who?
Carrie on with what you're doing, I'm at the wrong door.

Marisa Fiordalisi

Knock! Knock!
Who's there?
Anita.
Anita who?
Anita drink of water.

Jeffrey Dietrich

Animal Antics

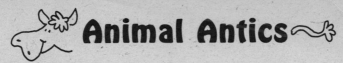

How do robins stay in shape?
They do worm-ups.

Melissa Rios

What is a bird after he is four days old?
Five days old.

Jamelle Denogean

How many hairs are in a rabbit's tail?
None. They are all on the outside.

Natalie Rose

What kind of bird do you hear when you eat?
A swallow.

Jenny Harris

Where do little cows go to eat?
The calf-eteria.

Aaron Butcher

Why can't bears fly?
Because they can't afford airline tickets.

Larry Story

How long should a rabbit's legs be?
Long enough to reach the ground.

Kellie Goettsche

Where do sheep get their hair cut?
At the baa-baa shop.

Jessica McKinney

Why is it cheap to feed a giraffe?
Because they make a little food go a long way.

Sarah Ray

There was a skunk named "In" and one named "Out." Once Out went in and In went out of a store. Then In's mother went in and said to Out, "Bring In in." So Out went out, got In, and both skunks went in. Then In's mother asked Out, "How did you find In so fast?" Out said, "Instincts." *Katy Andrew*

Around the Neighborhood

Who's bigger—Mr. Bigger or Mr. Bigger's baby?
Mr. Bigger's baby. He's a little bigger.

Amanda Cogbill

How can you tell if a tree is
a dogwood tree?
By its bark.

Jennifer Kucera

Why did the guy sleep under the car?
Because he wanted to wake up oily.

Brad Parsons

Why did the branch fall off the tree?
Because it wanted to leave.

Paul Cacici

How did the barber get to the shop so quickly?
He took a shortcut.

Matthew Croteau

What loses its head in the morning and gets it back at night?
A pillow.

Jason Trask

Why was the fire-eater absent from the circus?
Because he had very bad heartburn.

Jeff Caldwell

Why can't a bike stand up by itself?
Because it's two-tired.

Liz Phillips

Harry's mom had three boys. The first boy's name was Tom.
The second boy's name was David. What was the third boy's
name?
Harry.

Tina Potts

When is the best time to take a trip?
In the fall.

Ian Halsey

Did you hear the joke about the sidewalk?
It's all over town.

Amy McNeil

Why are people living on the opposite side of the road from a cemetery not allowed to be buried in that cemetery?
Because they're still living.

Aaron Vandiver

How is a baby like an old car?
Because it never goes anywhere without a rattle.

Danny Braxton

Why did the man throw the butter out the window?
Because he wanted to see the butterfly.

Carlton Reed

Why did the kids bring a baseball player along on their oamping trip?
Because they needed someone to pitch the tent.

Ryan Herald

What is the best way to make a fire with two sticks?
Make sure one of the sticks is a match.

Eddie Cox

Why did the girl eat bullets?
So her hair would come out in bangs.

Jenni Backe

If eight eggs cost twenty-six cents, how many eggs can you buy for a cent and a quarter?
Eight eggs.

Jennifer Stalvey

What is the best kind of mail to get in the summer?
Fan mail.

Erika Huyett

A boy fell off a 100-foot ladder and did not get hurt. How can this be?
He was on the first step.

Daniel Rose

Why does a fireman wear red suspenders?
To keep his pants up.
Dane Sherlock

1

Classroom Comedy

What are the school bully's favorite colors?
Black and blue.

Jerrod Perrine

What's the difference between a teacher and a train?
A train says "Chew-chew!" while a teacher says "Spit out the gum."

Gerilen Palmiere

Josh: My teacher said we're having a test today, rain or shine.
Erin: Then why are you so happy?
Josh: Because it's snowing.

Erin Walsh

Teacher: Chip, please use the word "arrest" in a sentence.
Chip: After riding up a steep hill, you're in need of arrest.

Keith Murphy

Why did the Cyclops have to close his school?
Because he only had one pupil.

Bethany Gilbert

Teacher: Class, when did the Great Depression start?
Student: Last week when I got my report card.

Kristen Anderson

Teacher: Where was the Declaration of Independence signed?
Student: At the bottom.

Amanda Butryn

Why did the boy tell everyone his grades were under water?
Because they were below C level.

Samira Hekmat

Student: But I don't think I deserve a zero on this paper.
Teacher: Neither do I, but it's the lowest grade I can give you.

Debbie Lyons

Teacher: Yes, Frank. What is it?
Frank: I don't want to scare you, but Dad said if I don't get better marks soon someone will be due for a spanking.

Danit Ariel

Teacher: Use the word "climate" in a sentence.
Student: I have a cherry tree in the backyard and my parents won't let me climate.

Michaela Bell

What is 7,089,006,889 and 91,108,988,910,718?
A math problem.

Garry Antunes

Why did the class clown eat the dollar he brought to school?
Because it was his lunch money.

Kristy Hudson

With tears in his eyes, the little boy told his kindergarten teacher that only one pair of boots was left in the classroom and they weren't his. The teacher searched and searched, but she couldn't find any other boots. "Are you sure these boots aren't yours?" she asked. "I'm sure," the little boy sobbed, "mine had snow on them."

Christen David

"Are you homesick?" the teacher asked a small girl on the first day of school. "No," replied the girl, "I'm here sick."

Jeremy Grillot

"I'm here sick!"

John: I went to the dentist this morning.
Teacher: Does your tooth still hurt?
John: I don't know. The dentist kept it.

Andreas Hatch

Teacher: Well, there's one good thing I can tell you about your son.
Father: Oh? What's that?
Teacher: With his grades, he can't possibly be cheating.

Casey Nestor

Wade: I think our school has a ghost in it.
Howard: Why?
Wade: Because our principal is always talking about our school spirit.

Wade Reaves

Teacher: Do you know Lincoln's Gettysburg Address?
Student: I thought he lived in the White House.

Carla Chinn

Why did the boy who always missed school always get A's?
Because he was never there to make any mistakes.

Hank Wolfe

◁🍴Menu, Please!🍴▷

Customer: What is the specialty of the house?
Waiter: No special tea. Everybody gets the same tea!

Elissa Guskin

Customer: Waiter, how come this sandwich is squashed?
Waiter: You told me to step on it.

Danny Zysman

Customer: Waiter, there's
a fly in my soup!
Waiter: Shh! Everyone
will want one.

Randy Petronio

A man walked into a restaurant and asked, "How much is a cup
of coffee?" The waiter said, "Fifty cents." Then the man asked,
"How much are refills?" The waiter said, "Refills are free."
So the man said, "I'll take a refill then."

Jim Ranieri

Customer: Is there any soup on the menu?
Waiter: There was, but I wiped it off.

Jon Meyers

Customer: What kind of pie is this—apple or peach?
Waiter: What does it taste like?
Customer: It tastes like glue.
Waiter: Then it must be apple. The peach tastes like paste.

Timmy Clark

A man walked into a restaurant, sat down and yelled, "Waiter!
Waiter! Do you serve crabs?" "Yes, we serve everyone," the
waiter replied.

Paul Bradley

Customer: I would like a pepperoni pizza.
Waitress: How many pieces would you like to have your pizza
   cut in—six or eight?
Customer: You better cut it in six. I don't think I can eat eight.

Andrea Ramezan

Customer: Waiter, why does this lobster have a missing leg?
Waiter: It was in a fight.
Customer: Well, take it back and bring me the winner.

Amanda Blain

Cross the Road

Why did the duck cross the road?
Because it was taped to the turkey.

Lynn Podlasek

Why did the cow cross the road?
Because the chicken was on vacation.

Anthony McMillon

Why did the peanut butter sandwich cross the road?
To get to the jelly side.

Charley Carey

Why did the rooster cross the road?
To prove he wasn't a chicken.

Aaron Acosta

Why did the turtle cross the road?
To get to the shell station.

Kelly Healy

Why did the chicken cross the road?
To prove to the opossum it could be done.

Katy Kleinpeter

Why didn't the orange cross the road?
Because it ran out of juice.

Keith Cramer

Why did the chicken cross the road?
Because the light turned green.

Kristina Marie Collins

Why did the turkey cross the road?
Because it was the chicken's day off.

Matt Bush

Why did the fox cross the road?
Because it was chasing the chicken.

Samantha Jo Cox

Why didn't the skeleton cross the road?
It didn't have the guts to.

Jason Webb

15

Have You Heard?

What did the salad dressing say to the refrigerator door?
"Close the door, I'm dressing!"

Olivia Davies

What did the motorcycle say after the man put gas in it?
"Tank you!"

Bert Coe

What did the sweater say to the lamb?
"Wool you be mine?"

Sasha Bournival

What kind of coat does a house wear?
A coat of paint.

Octavia Collie

Why did the doughnut shop close?
Because its owner got tired of the hole business.

June Kha

Where did Superman open a fast food restaurant?
On Lois Lane.

Jennifer Fabrizio

What's the difference between a monster and peanut butter?
A monster doesn't stick to the roof of your mouth.

Lona Suleiman

When is a door not a door?
When it's ajar.

Jennifer Miller

Customer: Can I put this wallpaper on myself?
Clerk: Sure, but it would look better on the wall.

Regenna Prine

What kind of trains carry bubble gum?
Chew-chew trains.

Kate Webster

16

This & That

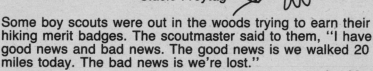

Why did the man count elephants instead of sheep when he was trying to go to sleep?
Because he was nearsighted.

Timothy O'Connell

Did you hear about the man who stayed up all night wondering where the sun had gone?
It finally dawned on him.

Stacie Freytag

Some boy scouts were out in the woods trying to earn their hiking merit badges. The scoutmaster said to them, "I have good news and bad news. The good news is we walked 20 miles today. The bad news is we're lost."

Jay Mangrum

Salesman: This new super computer can do half your job for you.
Business Executive: Great! I'll take two!

Sean Sutherland

First Person: What's the difference between a skunk and a dozen eggs?
Second Person: I don't know.
First Person: Well then, remind me never to send you out for eggs.

Eve Stenson

Anne: What is yellow and brown and has a hundred legs?
Susan: I don't know.
Anne: I don't know either, but it's crawling up your neck.

Chad Garrett

What school did Sir Lancelot go to?
Knight school.

Alton Polk

Ted: Did you know there was a kidnapping down the street?
Jerry: What happened?
Ted: His mother woke him up.

Suzanne Hayes

Why do elevators run up and down?
Because they're in too much of a hurry to walk.

Abigail Garcia

17

What Do You Get When...

What do you get when you put four ducks in a box?
A box of quackers.

Erica Wasil

What do you get when you drop a piano down a mine?
A flat miner.

Aaron Martin

What do you get when you cross a rooster and a giraffe?
An animal that can wake people on the top floor of a building.

Sean Amidon

What do you get when you cross a chicken and a bell?
An alarm cluck.

Tanya Ondish

What do you get when you find a four-leaf clover in a patch of poison ivy?
A rash of good luck.

Sadie McDowell

What do you get when you cross a turkey with a whale?
A Thanksgiving dinner that needs tons of stuffing.

Julie Cox

What do you get when you cross a pit bull with Lassie?
A dog that bites your leg off and then runs for help.

Brian Thiry

What do you get when you cross a pig with a pine tree?
A pork-u-pine.

Bjorn Hubbard

What do you get when you cross an owl and a goat?
A hootenanny.

Ashley Marie Keyes

What do you get when you cross a midget and a computer?
You get a short circuit.

Clayton Lassiter

What do you get when you cross a karate expert with a pig?
Pork chops.

Elizabeth Maglio

Silly Situations

Sam: Gee, I'm glad my
mother named me Sam.
Sally: Why?
Sam: 'Cause that's what
everyone calls me!
Jennifer Wood

**What did the baby computer
say when it got hurt?**
"I want my da-ta!"
Bethany Elam

Why did the chicken cross the road?
Because it wanted to get to the other side.

Jon Fries

Customer: What dishes do you have for me to eat?
Waiter (horrified): You eat dishes?

Aaron Adams

**I'm full when I'm gone, and I'm empty when I'm here.
What am I?**
A suitcase.

Veronica Dye

First Person: What would you do if you were in my shoes?
Second Person: Polish them.

Jonathon Kunkle

**When does a car look like
a frog?**
When it's being towed.
Michele Gibson

**What kind of pants do
ghosts wear?**
Boo jeans.

Kurt Runge

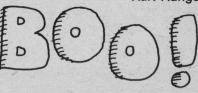

19

Hodgepodge

There was a lady who had 6 penguins in her car. A policeman pulled her over and said, "Take those penguins to the zoo." The lady said, "Okay, officer." Two weeks later, the same policeman pulled her over. The 6 penguins were still in the car, but now they were wearing sunglasses. The policeman said, "I thought I told you to take those penguins to the zoo." The lady said, "I did, and we had such a good time that now I'm taking them to the beach."

Laura Nolde

What did one fish say to the other fish after it was hooked?
"That's what you get for not keeping your mouth shut!"

Loretta McWilliams

What did the plate say to the spoon?
"Don't get too close to me, I have a dish-ease."

Celeste Ng

What did the light bulb say to the lamp?
"Turn me off, I'm burning up."

Michele Pomager

First Snake: I hope I'm not poisonous.
Second Snake: Why?
First Snake: I just bit my tongue. *Jennifer Sumcad*

Why did the baby snake cry?
Because it lost its rattle.

Andrea Lawson

Tim: Which hand do you eat with, your right or your left?
Tony: Neither. I use a spoon.

Johnny Ng

A boy went into a pet shop and asked the shopkeeper for 25 cents' worth of birdseed. "How many birds do you have?" asked the shopkeeper. "None," replied the boy, "I want to grow some."

Claunard Jean Baptiste

20

Customer: I've come to buy a car. I can't remember its name, but it starts with T.
Car Salesman: Sorry, we don't have any cars that start with tea. Ours all use gasoline.

Joey Wagner

Why don't teddy bears eat?
Because they're always stuffed.

Andre Hallman

What do teachers and eye doctors have in common?
They both test pupils.

Andy Orsillo

Why did the man only water half his lawn?
Because he heard there was a 50 percent chance of rain.

Scott Alexander

Why can't a bank keep secrets?
Because there are so many tellers.

James Pentland

Why did the man start digging up the railroad track?
He saw the X on the sign and thought he struck gold.

Bethany Asher

Man (in pet store): I want this bird. Send me the bill.
Clerk: Sorry, sir. You have to take the whole bird.

Penny Stone

George: I wish I had seven cents.
Joe: Why?
George: Then I'd only need three more cents to have a dime.

Jennifer Webb

A girl went to buy some long underwear. The man in the store asked how long she'd like them. The girl replied, "Oh, from about December to April."

Christy Carter

Frank: Have you ever seen a catfish?
Stan: Don't kid me, cats can't fish!

Paul Slavin

Why did the boy keep his shirt on when he took a bath?
Because the label said "wash and wear."

Kara Dobbin

More Riddles...

Jim: What has whiskers and a tail, washes itself with its tongue, catches mice, and barks like a dog?
Kim: I have no idea.
Jim: A cat.
Kim: But you said it barks like a dog.
Jim: I didn't want to make it too easy for you.

Todd Crews

What kind of keys cannot open doors?
Monkeys, donkeys, and turkeys.

Alison Loof

What is green, has 2 legs, and a trunk?
A seasick tourist.

Min Chu Yi

If you had a long candle, a short candle, and a medium candle, which would burn faster?
None of them. They all burn the same.

April Janita

**I have one. You have one.
I use yours more than you do.
You use mine more than I do.
What is it?**
Your name.

Edward Davis

What letters are not in the alphabet?
The ones in the mailbox.

Tonya Hughes

What can you do with a book, a pen, and a clock?
You can read a book, write with a pen, and tell time with a clock.

Stephanie Riggins

What's the ozone?
The place in the alphabet between n and p.

Matthew Sousa

How does a car feel after a long trip?
Exhausted.

DeAnna Jones

Which moves faster—heat or cold?
Heat, because you can catch cold.

Sharon Carpenter

When is a stick like a king?
When it is a ruler.

Andee Roberts

What is the laziest mountain in the world?
Mount Ever Rest.

Rachel Sheffield

He wears a red suit, carries a big black bag, and falls down chimneys. Who is he?
Santa Clutz.

Amber Dawn Ledbetter

What does a miser spend and a spendthrift save?
Nothing.

Jason Harmon

You have to get dressed to go to school, but the power went out. You don't have a flashlight. You have to get two matching socks out of your drawer. There are 10 red socks and 10 blue socks in the drawer. What is the least number of socks that you can take out of the drawer, knowing that you will have a matching pair?
Three.

Nickl Miller

What has three hundred feet, but no legs?
A football field.

Jason Pryor

Why is a dime smarter than a nickel?
Because it has more cents.

Stephanie Polce

Why did the girl put a bag of sugar under her pillow?
Because she wanted to have sweet dreams.

Benjamin Martin

Why did Humpty Dumpty have a great fall?
To make up for his crummy summer.

Derek Thomas

Good Guys & Bad Guys

Why was the belt arrested?
Because it held up a pair of pants.

Billy Lipscomb

What is the difference between a jailer and a jeweler?
One sells watches and the other watches cells.

Brandon Wiemiller

Why did the robber take a bath?
So he could make a clean getaway.

Eric Isaacson

What happened to the man who stole the calendar?
He got twelve months.

Nisnaka Toppin

Officer: Why didn't you stop when I blew my whistle?
Man: Well, I'm a little deaf.
Officer: Don't worry, here's a court summons. You'll get your hearing in the morning.

Tara Till

What did the defendant say when the judge yelled, "Order in the court!"?
"A large soda, and some fries to go."

Mike Watkins

A zookeeper was talking to three boys who were in trouble. He said, "Tell me your names and what you were doing." The first boy said, "Tommy. I was trying to feed peanuts to the lions." The second boy said, "Billy. I was trying to feed peanuts to the lions." The third boy said, "My name is Peanuts."

Tony Hahn

Why couldn't the spy talk clearly?
Because he had a code in his nose.

Mandy McAlister

How did the detective find the missing gray hair?
He combed through the evidence.

Steve Ellis

Judge: Have you ever been up before me?
Defendant: I don't know, what time do you get up?

Josh David Martin

Fiddle Faddles

What's more wonderful than a counting dog?
A spelling bee.

Holly Pappas

First Person: Who gave you those two black eyes?
Second Person: Nobody gave them to me. I had to fight
  for them.

Jason Emmen

There was a woman who wanted to take a bath in milk. So she
called the dairy and asked them to deliver some milk. The man
at the dairy asked, "Do you want it pasteurized?" The woman
replied, "No, just a little above the knees is fine."

Troy Robertson

When does Thursday come before Wednesday?
In the dictionary.

Daniele Phillips

How did the termites get into Wally's party?
In a chew-chew train.

Maria Flores

**If April showers bring May flowers, what do May flowers
bring?**
Pilgrims.

Kurt Meier

**What continent do you see
when you get up and look
in the mirror?**
You see Europe!

Vestal Odom

Have a
nice twip!

What is a twip?
What a wabbit takes when
it wides a twain.

Ashley Wells

Would You Believe?

What always goes up but never comes down?
Your age.

Cristie Zack

Why was the letter damp?
Because the postage was due.

Carmen Hickman

Why is up up and down down?
Because if up was down and down was up, everyone would be confused.

Michael Zito

What can you put in a barrel to make it lighter?
A hole.

Courtney Galla

What happened twice in America and Asia?
The letter A.

Noel Arthur

What two letters do teeth hate the most?
DK.

Thomas DiNuzzo

Why don't fish play tennis?
Because they're afraid they might get caught in the net.

Joey Orca

What is green and keeps its heart in its head?
A head of lettuce.

Brian Leatham

What never asks questions but always has to be answered?
The telephone.

David Beals

What should you do when a rabbit is eating your dictionary?
Take the words right out of its mouth.

Wesley Medina

What kind of trees come in two?
Pear trees.

Ryan Wolfe

What's worse than finding a worm in your apple?
Finding half a worm.

Ryan Conroy

What's red and eats peanuts?
An embarrassed elephant.
Jennifer McConnell

Why can't a hand be 12 inches?
Because then it would be a foot.
Eric Bucklew

What is the best time to tell scary stories?
When the spirit moves you.
Lorlece McMasters

What can run but has no legs?
Water.

J.J. Kelly

Why did Santa go to the English class?
Because he wanted to learn about Clauses.

Alison Reese

What goes snap, crackle, fizz?
A lightning bug with a short circuit.

Sherie Snellgrove

What is the longest word in the world?
Smiles, because there's a mile between the s's.
Phillip Hutcherson

Why is a bridge like money?
Because they both go bank to bank.

Sammie DePasse

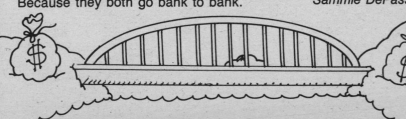

27

Knock! Knock!

Knock! Knock!
Who's there?
Pencil.
Pencil who?
Pencil fall down if
you don't wear a belt.

Rachel Farber

Knock! Knock!
Who's there?
Want.
Want who?
Want to hear another knock-knock joke?

Kourtney Hensley

Knock! Knock!
Who's there?
Cows go.
Cows go who?
Cows go moo, not who.

Janet Pontious

Knock! Knock!
Who's there?
Rabbit.
Rabbit who?
Rabbit up nicely, it's a present.

Shayla Maria Inez Taylor

Ring! Ring!
Who's there?
Hurd.
Hurd who?
Hurd my hand, can't knock.

Stephanie Deskins

Knock! Knock!
Who's there?
Turnip.
Turnip who?
Turnip the radio—
I can't hear it.

Sasha Roden

Who's There?

Knock! Knock!
Who's there?
Eileen.
Eileen who?
Eileen on your doorbell, but it doesn't ring.

Meri Patrick

Knock! Knock!
Who's there?
Boo.
Boo who?
Don't cry, it's only a joke.

Andrea Carrico

Knock! Knock!
Who's there?
Bayou.
Bayou who?
Bayou a sandwich if you buy me a soda.

Jay Perkins

Knock! Knock!
Who's there?
A-1.
A-1 who?
A-1 to suck your blood.

Heather Irwin

Knock! Knock!
Who's there?
Orange.
Orange who?
Orange you glad to see me?

Paul Raggo

Knock! Knock!
Who's there?
Gorilla.
Gorilla who?
Gorilla me a hamburger, I'm hungry.
Molly Gammon

Kitty Corner

When is it bad luck to have a black cat *follow* you?
When you're a mouse.
Brennan Taylor

Why did the cat join the Red Cross?
Because it wanted to be a first aid kit.

Ali Neal

Where will the cat be when the lights go out?
In the dark.
Brian Rogers

There was a boat full of ten cats. One jumped out. How many were left?
None, they were all copycats.
Nancy Browne

Which animal has more lives than a cat?
A frog because it croaks every night.

Taffini Ann Nespodzany

What did the cat say when it stepped on the tack?
"Me-ouch!"

Jennifer Willey

Why was the cat arrested?
Because it was caught committing a *mouse*demeanor.

Tyke Parrish

What does a 500 lb. mouse say to a cat?
"Here kitty, kitty!"

Michael Markarian

What is a cat's favorite color?
Purr-ple.

Thomas Mims

What is a cat's favorite play?
Ro-*meow* and Juliet.

Melissa McIntosh

Things That Go Bump

How do witches on broomsticks drink their tea?
Out of flying saucers.

Matt Kain

Why didn't the teacher believe the little ghost's excuses?
Because she could see right through them.

Jessica Mercier

What does a little ghost call his mother and father?
His transparents.

Lisa Oakes

Why don't mummies go on vacation?
Because they're afraid they might relax and unwind.

Ray Convy

First Person: Have you seen the invisible man?
Second Person: No, but I heard he was out of sight.

Michelle Turgeon

What body of water do ghosts like best?
Lake Erie.

Rodney Zimmerman

Two boys were standing in front of a mummy case at a museum. The case said 1275 B.C. "I wonder what 1275 B.C. means," said the first boy. The second boy thought for a moment, then said, "It must be the license plate number of the car that hit him!"

Jacqueline Casto

Which contest did the witch's broom win?
The sweepstakes.

Allison Brown

What is a ghost's favorite road?
A dead end.

Tammy Madsen

Why do witches
ride brooms?
Because vacuum
cleaners are too heavy.
Dana Vosbeck

31

Assorted Sports

**Why did Cinderella's
baseball team always lose?**
Because her coach was a pumpkin.
Amanda Gosselin

How does a football player go fishing?
With his tackle.

Christopher Bright

Why is a baseball team like a pancake?
Because they both need a good batter.

Robby Cain

Why is it so hot in the stadium after a football game?
Because all the fans have left.

Jess Taylor

Why should you never tell a joke while you're ice skating?
Because the ice might crack up.

Shaun Gainforth

**Two teams were playing baseball. Team A won without a
single man crossing over first base. How could this be?**
They were all married.

Heather Turner

What is the hardest thing about learning how to skate?
The ground.

Stephanie Elmore

Why do the greatest baseball players wear masks?
So they can steal bases without being recognized.

Giniffer Stoffer

Why is tennis such a noisy game?
Because each player raises a racket.

Misty Dawn Hall

What baseball player holds the drinks?
The pitcher.

John Tucker

Why does a golfer wear two pairs of socks?
In case he gets a hole in one.

Michael Gaspar

Around the House

Son: Dad, may I have a dime?
Father: Don't you think you're getting a little too old for dimes?
Son: You're right, Dad! How about a dollar?

Dennell Joyner

Mother: Why does your room look like a tornado hit it?
Son: Because I just had a brainstorm.

Steven Reynaga

Son: Mommy, I just knocked over the ladder in the backyard.
Mother: Well, you'd better tell your father.
Son: He already knows. He was on it.

Marlene Plank

Son: Mom, I'm going outside to play football.
Mother: With your new jeans?
Son: No, with the kid next door.

Matt Canady

What always comes into the house through the keyhole?
A key.

Erin Jones

Danny: I'm not going back to school.
Mother: Why not?
Danny: Because on Monday my teacher said, "5 + 5 = 10." On Tuesday she said, "6 + 4 = 10." Today she said, "8 + 2 = 10." I'm not going back until she makes up her mind.

Lisa Estep

Son: Mom, I got a 100 in school today.
Mother: Wow, that's great! In what subject?
Son: A 40 in math and a 60 in English.

Johanna Fisher

Why did the boy put the banana peel in his bed?
So he could slip out of bed in the morning.

Stacy Davis

Father: What did you learn in school today, son?
Boy: We learned how to say "Yes, sir" and "Yes, ma'am."
Father: You did?
Boy: Yup.

Curtis Hulliger

33

Did You Hear...?

What did the clock maker say to the broken clock?
"We have ways of making you tock."

Jovannie Lorenzo

What did the picture say to the wall?
"First they frame me, then they hang me."

Tina Plerhoples

What did one eye say to the other eye?
"There's something in the middle that smells."

Joey Brockway

What did the little light bulb say to its mother?
"I wuv you watts and watts."

Pamela Brandt

What did the ocean say to the beach?
Nothing. It just waved.

Morgan Broderick

What did one pretzel say to the other pretzel?
"Let's twist!"

Nancy Vislocky

What did the big hose say to the little hose?
"Hi, squirt."

Bonnie Fair

What does an envelope say when you lick it?
Nothing. It just shuts up.

Dawn Ghisu

What did one pie say to the other pie?
"I think I've got a crust on you!"

Barry Kraus

What did one candle say to the other candle?
"Are you going out tonight?"

Kelly Harvey

What did the seamstress say when she made a mistake?
"Sew what?"

Loretta Birkholz

What did the apple say to the sick banana?
"How ya peeling?"

Erin Uker

What did one flea say to the other flea?
"Should we walk or take the dog?"

Christie Caire

What did the beaver say to the tree?
"It's been nice gnawing you."

Kathlene Richardson

What did one strawberry say to the other strawberry?
"If you weren't so fresh, we wouldn't be in such a big jam."

Nicole Combs

What were Eli Whitney's famous last words?
"Keep your cotton pickin' hands off my cotton gin."

Amy Rioc

What did the boy volcano say to the girl volcano?
"Do you lava me like I lava you?"

John Rimmer

What did the bald man say when he got a comb for his birthday?

"Thank you. I'll never part with it."

Kelly Lenaghan

thanks a lot!

What did the fork say to the knife?
"You're looking sharp!"

Suzanne Ricci

What did the judge say to the dentist?
"Do you swear to pull the tooth, the whole tooth, and nothing but the tooth?"

Rebecca Blocksome

What did the limestone say to the geologist?
"Stop taking me for granite."

Leslie Hester

What did one tree say to the other tree?
"Leaf me alone."

Jenny Zimmerman

...And More Riddles

If a man smashed a clock, could he be accused of killing time?
Not if the clock struck first.

Julie Phelan

What travels a lot during the day, playing and running, comes home at night and stays in the corner with its tongue hanging out?
Your shoe.

Robert Massey

As I was walking across London Bridge, I met a man. He tipped his cap, and drew his cane, and in this riddle I said his name. What is it?
Andrew.

Cindy Johnson

Where does the President keep his armies?
In his sleevies.

Alicia Lipke

What's a sure way to get into the circus?
Buy a ticket.

Reid Kim

Did you hear the joke about the unsharpened pencil?
It didn't have a point.

William Springer

Why do you go to bed at night?
Because the bed won't come to you.

Zack Kimball

Which clown wears the biggest shoes?
The one with the biggest feet.

Jose Hernandez

How is the letter A like a flower?
There's a B after it.

Eun Sung Jang

Doggie Deeds

A man went to the movies, and was very surprised to find a lady with a large dog sitting in front of him. What he found even more surprising was that the dog laughed at every funny part in the comedy. "Excuse me," the man said, "but I think it's amazing that your dog likes the movie as much as he does." The lady looked at him and said, "I'm just as surprised as you are. He hated the book."

Cathy Elmer

What's a good way to keep a dog off the street?
Put him in a barking lot.

Lindsey Diers

What did the shaggy dog do when a man-eating tiger was following him?
Nothing. It was a man-eating tiger, not a shaggy-dog eating one.

Josh Rocko Slattery

Where do dogs hate going?
To flea markets.

Steven Milvet

What does a dog do after he's done performing?
He takes a bow-wow.

Priscilla Schaeffer

What do you call a dog that stays out in the cold?
A chilly dog.

Christina Taylor

Bo: Does your dog have a license?
Bob: No. He's not old enough to drive yet.
Josh Conner

When is a dog's tail like a farmer's cart?
When it's a waggin'.

Anthony Amaral

When is a sheepdog most likely to go into a house?
When the door is open.
Stacey Bawden

Ruff!

What did the dog say when he sat on the sandpaper?
"Ruff!"

Amanda Berg

Whatchamacallit?

What do you call a boy who doesn't have any nickels?
Nicholas.

Brad Boyd

What do you call a bear that rides a horse without a saddle?
A bearback rider.

Sara Larson

What do you call it when a shaggy dog is launched into outer space?
A hair-raising experience.

Rhonda Lynn Keaton

What do you call a fast duck?
A quick quack.

Michael Kelso

What do you call a grandfather clock?
An old-timer.

Bobby Long

What do you call a chicken that goes across the road, rolls in the dirt and comes back across?
A dirty double-crosser.

Aisha Iturralde

What do you call a skeleton that rings doorbells?
A dead ringer.

Christian Barnes

What do you call the author of a Western story book?
A horseback writer.

William Kauffman

What do you call an oyster that won't give up its pearl?
A selfish shellfish.

Amy Cote

What do you call little bugs that live on the moon?
Luna-ticks.

Mark Engengro

What do you call a picture of a cat painted by another cat?
A paw-trait.
Margaret Otterstrom

What do you call a stingy bird?
A cheap cheep.
Angie Robles

What's another name for a box lunch?
A square meal.
Shawn Allen Jackson

What do you call a pig that knows karate?
A pork chop.
Neil Reaves

What do you call 1,000 rabbits moving backwards?
A receding hare line.
Lance Blackstock

What do you call an ice cream truck man?
A sundae driver.
Jenny Forte

What do you call a cow with no legs?
Ground beef.
Shanna Hiatt

What do you call an adult balloon?
A blown-up.
Rachone Finnell

What do you call a bull when it is sleeping?
A bull-dozer.
Amanda Ryan

What do you call a croissant on roller skates?
Breakfast to go.
Kari Pinnekamp

Corny Knock-Knocks

Knock! Knock!
Who's there?
Needle.
Needle who?
Needle little money for the movies.

Sasha Harper

Knock! Knock!
Who's there?
Dewy.
Dewy who?
Dewy have to keep telling these knock-knock jokes?

Alyssa Bruce

Knock! Knock!
Who's there?
Yule.
Yule who?
Yule see.

Erin Garrett

Knock! Knock!
Who's there?
Little old lady.
Little old lady who?
I didn't know you could yodel.

Aspen Brunk

Little old lady who?

Knock! Knock!
Who's there?
Tarzan.
Tarzan who?
Tarzan stripes forever.
                    Angela Wallenstein

A Special Thanks To:

Acosta, Aaron, 10, Palm Vista Elem., 29 Palms, CA
Adams, Aaron, 7, Andover Elem., Andover, KS
Alexander, Scott, 10, Liberty School, Orland Park, IL
Amaral, Anthony, 10, Old County Road School, Esmond, RI
Amidon, Sean, 11, Moon Lake Elem., New Port Richey, FL
Anderson, Kristen, 10, Galena Middle, Galena, IL
Andrew, Katy, 9, Mint Valley Elem., Longview, WA
Antunes, Garry, 8, Westwood Primary, Palestine, TX
Ariel, Danit, 9, Balboa Street Magnet School, Northridge, CA
Arthur, Noel, 11, Blessed Sacrament School, Bronx, NY
Asher, Bethany, 11, Kramer Middle, Willimantic, CT
Backe, Jenni, 8, Timothy Ball Elem., Crown Point, IN
Baptiste, Claunard Jean, 10, St. Benedict Joseph Labre School,
   Richmond Hill, NY
Barnes, Christian, 8, Park School, Munhall, PA
Bawden, Stacey, 9, Castle Heights Elem., Price, UT
Beals, David, 10, Grand Terrace Elem., Colton, CA
Bell, Michaela, 11, Holy Family School, Mason City, IA
Berg, Amanda, 8, Larimore Elem., Larimore, ND
Birkholz, Loretta, 11, Lincoln Elem., Osage, IA
Blackstock, Lance, 11, Blackburn Elem., Independence, MO
Blain, Amanda, 9, Beale Elem., Gallipolis Ferry, WV
Blocksome, Rebecca, 8, Ransom Grade School, Ransom, KS
Boothe, Natasha, 7, Wallace Elem., Bristol, VA
Boulden, Eileen, 8, Larimore Elem., Larimore, ND
Bournival, Sasha, 9, St. Francis School, Manchester, NH
Boyd, Brad, 8, Paradise Elem., Paradise, PA
Bradley, Paul, 8, Liberty School, Scottsdale, AZ
Brandt, Pamela, 7, Stanwood School, New Stanton, PA
Braxton, Danny, 11, Lincoln-Roosevelt School, Succasunna, NJ
Bright, Christopher, 6, Oceanway Elem., Jacksonville, FL
Brockway, Joey, 9, Stella Niagara Educational Park, Stella Niagara, NY
Broderick, Morgan, 6, Tamanend Elem., Warrington, PA
Brown, Allison, 8, Lenox School, Portland, OR
Browne, Nancy, 8, Dearborn Heights School, Oak Lawn, IL
Bruce, Alyssa, 8, Washington Elem., Sapulpa, OK
Brunk, Aspen, 9, Centennial Elem., Loveland, CO
Bucklew, Eric, 8, Christ the King School, Pleasant Hill, CA

Burns, Carrie, 9, Huckleberry Hill Elem., Brookfield, CT
Bush, Matt, 9, Berryton Elem., Berryton, KS
Busser, Heather, 8, T.R. Davis School, Dollar Bay, MI
Butcher, Aaron, 6, St. Gregory School, Tyler, TX
Butryn, Amanda, 11, McKinley Intermediate, Lackawanna, NY
Cacici, Paul, 7, A.C. Whelan School, Revere, MA
Cain, Robby, 6, Van Zant School, Marlton, NJ
Caire, Christie, 7, Our Lady Star of the Sea School, New Orleans, LA
Caldwell, Jeff, 10, Hoxie Grade School, Hoxie, KS
Canady, Matt, 10, Sycamore School, Kokomo, IN
Carey, Charley, 7, Lura Sharp Elem., Pulaski, NY
Carpenter, Sharon, 8, Watson Elem., Huntsville, AR
Carrico, Andrea, 9, Wilson Elem., Sanford, FL
Carter, Christy, 7, Erskine School, Cedar Rapids, IA
Casto, Jacqueline, 11, La Union Elem., Anthony, NM
Cearfoss, Scott, 11, Busansky School, Pemberton, NJ
Chinn, Carla, 9, Western Branch Elem., Chesapeake, VA
Clark, Susan Ailene, 10, Palm Vista Elem., 29 Palms, CA
Clark, Timmy, 11, Stanley Elem., Stanley, KY
Coe, Bert, 9, Gordon McCaw Elem., Henderson, NV
Cogbill, Amanda, 8, Jimmy Brown Elem., Star City, AR
Coles, Krystal, 11, La Union Elem., Anthony, NM
Collie, Octavia, 8, Opa Locka Elem., Opa Locka, FL
Collins, Kevin, 11, St. Thomas School, Sanford, ME
Collins, Kristina Marie, 11, Eugene Field School, Webb City, MO
Combs, Nicole, 11, Our Lady of Mercy School, Baton Rouge, LA
Conner, Josh, 9, Elizabeth School, Shelby, NC
Conroy, Ryan, 8, Park School, Munhall, PA
Convy, Ray, 11, Salem Middle, Richmond, VA
Cote, Amy, 10, Radburn School, Fair Lawn, NJ
Cox, Eddie, 11, Augusta Raa Middle, Tallahassee, FL
Cox, Julie, 8, Happy Valley Elem., Glasgow, KY
Cox, Samantha Jo, 8, Enochville School, China Grove, NC
Cramer, Keith, 8, Liberty School, Scottsdale, AZ
Crews, Todd, 9, William Yates Elem., Independence, MO
Croteau, Matthew, 7, Primary School, Leicester, MA
David, Christen, 9, Mandeville Middle, Mandeville, LA
Davies, Olivia, Grade 4, McDonogh School, Owings Mills, MD
Davis, Edward, 8, West Oxford School, Oxford, NC
Davis, Stacy, Grade 2, South Cumberland Elem., Crossville, TN
Denogean, Jamelle, 9, Palm Vista Elem., 29 Palms, CA
DePasse, Sammie, 9, North Elem., Marshall, IL
Deskins, Stephanie, 10, Tazewell Elem., Tazewell, VA
Diers, Lindsey, 7, Erskine School, Cedar Rapids, IA
Dietrich, Jeffrey, 9, Lake Placid Elem., Lake Placid, NY
DiNuzzo, Thomas, 7, Park Avenue School, Westbury, NY
Dobbin, Kara, 7, Erskine School, Cedar Rapids, IA
Durre, Jennifer, 11, Flanagan Jr. High, Flanagan, IL
Dye, Veronica, 7, Reagan Magnet School, Odessa, TX
Elam, Bethany, 6, Carolyn Wenz School, Paris, IL
Ellis, Steve, 11, Walton Elem., Walton, WV
Elmer, Cathy, 11, St. Joseph School, Mendham, NJ
Elmore, Stephanie, 7, Lincoln Park School, Knoxville, TN

Emmen, Jason, 9, Palm Vista Elem., 29 Palms, CA
Engelbrecht, Jennifer, 11, Augusta Raa Middle, Tallahassee, FL
Engengro, Mark, 8, Saint Stephen School, Hamden, CT
Estep, Lisa, 11, Triplett Middle, Mount Jackson, VA
Evans, Kathryn Margaret, 9, Colton Pierrepont Central, Colton, NY
Fabrizio, Jennifer, 10, St. Benedict Joseph Labre School,
   Richmond Hill, NY
Fair, Bonnie, 8, St. Elizabeth Elem., Pittsburgh, PA
Fairley, Katina, 11, Collins Middle, Collins, MS
Farber, Rachel, 10, Hoxie Grade School, Hoxie, KS
Finnell, Rachone, 7, Emporia Elem., Emporia, VA
Fiordalisi, Marisa, 10, Vernon Middle, East Norwich, NY
Fisher, Johanna, 9, East Salem School, Salem, VA
Fitzgerald, Shannon, 10, St. Michael School, Livonia, MI
Flores, Maria, 10, Ranchwood Elem., Yukon, OK
Fornoff, Krystal, 9, New Central School, Havana, IL
Forte, Jenny, Grade 2, E.N. Nordgaard Elem., Glenwood, MN
Freytag, Stacie, 9, Academy Elem., Temple, TX
Fries, Jon, 10, Blessed Trinity School, Ocala, FL
Gainforth, Shaun, 9, Unionville Elem., Unionville, MI
Galla, Courtney, 10, Wading River Elem., Wading River, NY
Gammon, Molly, Grade 1, Nevada Community School, Nevada, IA
Garcia, Abigail, 7, Ajo Elem., Ajo, AZ
Garrett, Chad, 8, Flint River Academy, Woodbury, GA
Garrett, Erin, 9, Lenox School, Portland, OR
Gaspar, Michael, 9, Windmill Street School, Providence, RI
Ghisu, Dawn, 10, St. Callistus School, Philadelphia, PA
Gibson, Michele, 11, Franklin School, Mattoon, IL
Gilbert, Bethany, 9, Killingly Central, Dayville, CT
Goettsche, Kellie, 10, Engleman School, Grand Island, NE
Gosselin, Amanda, 8, Round School, Hartland, MI
Gould, Tom, 9, Kaneland Elem., Maple Park, IL
Grande, Matthew, 10, Vernon Middle, East Norwich, NY
Grillot, Jeremy, 8, Bradford Elem., Bradford, OH
Groce, Jessica, 7, R. Elisabeth Maclary Primary, Newark, DE
Guskin, Elissa, 9, Old Bethpage Grade School, Old Bethpage, NY
Hahn, Tony, 11, North Decatur Elem., Greensburg, IN
Hall, Misty Dawn, 6, Northside Elem., Siloam Springs, AR
Hallman, Andre, 9, Opa Locka Elem., Opa Locka, FL
Halsey, Ian, 9, Hueytown Elem., Hueytown, AL
Harmon, Jason, 8, New Prospect Elem., Inman, SC
Harper, Sasha, 9, Roy Waldron Middle, La Vergne, TN
Harris, Jenny, 8, Pekin Elem., Packwood, IA
Harvey, Kelly, 6, Cedar Hill School, Towaco, NJ
Hatch, Andreas, 7, Neary School, Southborough, MA
Hayes, Suzanne, 10, New Washington Elem., New Washington, IN
Healy, Kelly, 10, Blessed Trinity School, Ocala, FL
Hekmat, Samira, 11, Fairburn Avenue School, Los Angeles, CA
Hensley, Kourtney, 8, Munson Primary, Mulvane, KS
Herald, Ryan, 8, Crothersville Elem., Crothersville, IN
Hernandez, Jose, 12, La Union Elem., Anthony, NM
Hester, Leslie, 8, Newport Elem., Newport, NC
Hiatt, Shanna, 7, White Plains School, White Plains, NC

Hickman, Carmen, 5, Grove Elem., Montrose, IL
Hubbard, Bjorn, 7, Kitty Stone Elem., Jacksonville, AL
Hudson, Kristy, 8, Central Park Elem., Bossier City, LA
Hughes, Tonya, 9, Fair Grove School, Thomasville, NC
Hulliger, Curtis, 9, Federalsburg Elem., Federalsburg, MD
Hutcherson, Phillip, 9, East Prairie School, Tuscola, IL
Huyett, Erika, 7, Alburtis School, Alburtis, PA
Irwin, Heather, 8, Wernert Elem., Toledo, OH
Isaacson, Eric, 8, Howe Avenue School, Sacramento, CA
Iturralde, Aisha, 8, P.S. 250, Brooklyn, NY
Jackson, Aaron, 8, Carlisle Elem., Carlisle, IA
Jackson, Shawn Allen, 11, Goose Rock Elem., Manchester, KY
Jang, Eun Sung, 8, Saipan Community School, Saipan, MP
Janita, April, 10, St. Odilia School, Shoreview, MN
Johnson, Cindy, 11, Tunica Institute of Learning, Tunica, MS
Jones, DeAnna, Grade 4, Roy Waldron Middle, La Vergne, TN
Jones, Erin, 9, S.M. Seabourn Elem., Mesquite, TX
Joyner, Dennell, 11, Salem Middle, Richmond, VA
Kain, Matt, 10, Unionville Elem., Unionville, MI
Kauffman, William, 8, Forbes Road Elem., Harrisonville, PA
Keaton, Rhonda Lynn, Grade 4, Booker T. Washington School,
   Lexington, KY
Kelly, J.J., 8, St. Elizabeth Elem., Pittsburgh, PA
Kelso, Michael, 7, Sunburst School, Glendale, AZ
Keyes, Ashley Marie, 7, Sacred Heart School, Pittsfield, MA
Kha, June, 9, Paradise Elem., Paradise, PA
Kim, Reid, 7, Ahuimanu Elem., Kaneohe, HI
Kimball, Zack, 9, Centennial Elem., Loveland, CO
Kleinpeter, Katy, 11, Our Lady of Mercy School, Baton Rouge, LA
Komisin, Mike, 7, Bartman Elem., Hermitage, PA
Kraus, Barry, 9, C.J. Davenport School, Cardiff, NJ
Kucera, Jennifer, 9, Westgate Elem., Omaha, NE
Kunkle, Jonathon, 10, Immaculate Conception School, Irwin, PA
Larson, Sara, Grade 3, Mohawk Trails Elem., Carmel, IN
Lassiter, Clayton, 8, Newport Elem., Newport, NC
Lawson, Andrea, 7, Stoneleigh Elem., Baltimore, MD
Leatham, Brian, 8, St. Timothy's School, Apple Valley, CA
Ledbetter, Amber Dawn, 8, Converse School, Beloit, WI
Lenaghan, Kelly, 10, St. Michael School, Livonia, MI
Lewis, Jackie, 9, Cotton Valley Elem., Cotton Valley, LA
Lipke, Alicia, Grade 3, Brooks School, Lewistown, MT
Lipscomb, Billy, 11, Flemington Elem., Flemington, WV
Lomax, Chris, 9, Falling Creek Elem., Elberton, GA
Long, Bobby, 8, Wakefield Elem., Wakefield, NE
Loof, Alison, 9, Pyrtle School, Lincoln, NE
Lorenzo, Jovannie, 8, P.S. 250, Brooklyn, NY
Lyons, Debbie, 9, Balboa Street Magnet School, Northridge, CA
Madsen, Tammy, 10, Castle Dale Elem., Castle Dale, UT
Maglio, Elizabeth, 11, Orfordville Elem., Orfordville, WI
Manbeck, LaTosha, 6, Travis School, El Paso, TX
Mangrum, Jay, 11, Kaiser Elem., Houston, TX
Markarian, Michael, 8, F.J. McGrath School, Worchester, MA
Martin, Aaron, 9, Woodbridge Elem., Tampa, FL

Martin, Benjamin, 8, Garland Christian Academy, Garland, TX
Martin, Josh David, 8, Park View Elem., Moundsville, WV
Massey, Robert, 6, Shannon Elem., Shannon, MS
McAlister, Mandy, 9, Falling Creek Elem., Elberton, GA
McConnell, Jennifer, 8, Log Pile School, Washington, PA
McDowell, Sadie, 7, Erskine School, Cedar Rapids, IA
McIntosh, Melissa, 7, Maple Street Elem., Hudson Falls, NY
McKenzie, Brian, 8, West Cedar Elem., Waverly, IA
McKinney, Jessica, 6, Trantwood Elem., Virginia Beach, VA
McMasters, Loriece, 10, Penns Manor Elem., Clymer, PA
McMillon, Anthony, 7, Belmont Elem., N. Babylon, NY
McNeil, Amy, 7, McNair School, Hazelwood, MO
McWilliams, Loretta, 7, Cobb Mt. Elem., Cobb, CA
Medina, Wesley, 8, Waggoner School, Winters, CA
Meier, Kurt, 9, Liberty School, Orland Park, IL
Mercier, Jessica, 7, Primary School, Leicester, MA
Meyers, Jon, Grade 2, Pine Tree Elem., Longview, TX
Miller, Jennifer, 10, Franklin School, Mattoon, IL
Miller, Nicki, 10, Clover Middle, Clover, SC
Miller, Noah, 9, Liberty School, Orland Park, IL
Milvet, Steven, 10, St. Joseph School, Mogadore, OH
Mims, Thomas, 9, Dunbar Elem., Ramer, AL
Moyet, Yvonne, 10, St. Benedict Joseph Labre School,
  Richmond Hill, NY
Mullins, John, 10, Ranchwood Elem., Yukon, OK
Murphy, Keith, 9, St. Clare School, Staten Island, NY
Murphy, Tommy, 7, Flint River Academy, Woodbury, GA
Neal, Ali, 9, Augusta Christian School, Martinez, GA
Nespodzany, Taffini Ann, 10, Northview School, Howards Grove, WI
Nestor, Casey, 9, Newport Elem., Newport, NC
Ng, Celeste, 8, Broughton Elem., Pittsburgh, PA
Ng, Johnny, 8, P.S. 250, Brooklyn, NY
Nolde, Laura, 10, St. Clare School, Staten Island, NY
O'Connell, Timothy, 10, Henry Barnard School, Enfield, CT
Oakes, Lisa, 8, Primary School, Leicester, MA
Odom, Vestal, 10, Annaville Elem., Corpus Christi, TX
Ohia, Okwuoma, 8, St. Elizabeth Elem., Pittsburgh, PA
Ondish, Tanya, 8, Edith M. Decker School, Mt. Arlington, NJ
Orca, Joey, 9, Washington Elem., Hawthorne, CA
Orsillo, Andy, 11, Augusta Raa Middle, Tallahassee, FL
Otterstrom, Margaret, 10, Holland Hall School, Tulsa, OK
Palmiere, Gerilen, 8, Immaculate Conception School, Pittsburgh, PA
Pappas, Holly, 9, Roosevelt School, Peru, IL
Parrish, Tyke, 8, McNair School, Hazelwood, MO
Parsons, Brad, 9, Kingston Elem., Kingston, MA
Patrick, Meri, 10, Hazle Elem., Hazleton, PA
Pedersen, Michael, 10, Vernon Middle, East Norwich, NY
Pentland, James, 10, Sacred Heart School, Dover, NJ
Perkins, Jay, 9, Cotton Valley Elem., Cotton Valley, LA
Perrine, Jerrod, 10, Alice Schafer Elem., Linesville, PA
Petersen, Wesley, 10, Palm Vista Elem., 29 Palms, CA
Petrecca, Linda, 9, Southwood Elem., Old Bridge, NJ
Petronio, Randy, 10, Alice Schafer Elem., Linesville, PA

Phelan, Julie, 8, Salina Elem., Salina, OK
Phillips, Daniele, 11, Lynchburg Elem., Lynchburg, TN
Phillips, Liz, 10, St. Odilia School, Shoreview, MN
Pinnekamp, Kari, 10, Wimbledon Courtenay School, Wimbledon, ND
Plank, Marlene, 7, Liberty Elem., Liberty, PA
Plerhoples, Tina, 8, Severn School, Corning, NY
Podlasek, Lynn, 10, Liberty School, Orland Park, IL
Polce, Stephanie, 9, Windmill Street School, Providence, RI
Polk, Alton, 8, Crescentwood School, East Detroit, MI
Pomager, Michele, 10, St. Christopher School, Philadelphia, PA
Pontious, Janet, 9, Galesburg School, Galesburg, KS
Posegate, Sarah, 8, Edith M. Decker School, Mt. Arlington, NJ
Potts, Tina, 10, Hamilton Elem., Hamilton, MO
Prine, Regenna, 10, York School, Springfield, MO
Pryor, Jason, 11, O.P. Earle Elem., Landrum, SC
Radford, Melissa, 7, St. Elizabeth School, Ozone Park, NY
Raggo, Paul, 7, Bismarck R-5 School, Bismarck, MO
Ramezan, Andrea, 9, Wilsonburg Grade School, Clarksburg, WV
Ramon, Denise, 9, Palm Vista Elem., 29 Palms, CA
Ranieri, Jim, 10, Blessed Trinity School, Ocala, FL
Ray, Sarah, 8, Kilby Elem., Woodbridge, VA
Reaves, Neil, 8, Kitty Stone Elem., Jacksonville, AL
Reaves, Wade, 10, C.G. Credle School, Oxford, NC
Reed, Carlton, 9, Lexington Elem., Monroe, LA
Reese, Alison, 10, St. Anne School, Bethlehem, PA
Reynaga, Steven, 10, Vaughn Street School, San Fernando, CA
Ricci, Suzanne, 7, Lynnhurst School, Saugus, MA
Rice, Amy, 11, Our Lady of Mercy School, Baton Rouge, LA
Richardson, Kathlene, 9, Mandeville Middle, Mandeville, LA
Riggins, Stephanie, 11, Western Branch Elem., Chesapeake, VA
Rimmer, John, 8, King Springs Elem., Smyrna, GA
Rios, Melissa, 7, St. Elizabeth School, Ozone Park, NY
Roberts, Andee, Grade 2, Acorn School, Mena, AR
Robertson, Troy, 9, Norris Elem., Omaha, NE
Robles, Angie, 8, Ricardo Elem., Kingsville, TX
Roden, Sasha, 8, Purdy Elem., Purdy, MO
Rogers, Brian, 7, Valley Park School, Cedar Falls, IA
Rosario, Jessica, 9, St. Benedict Joseph Labre School,
  Richmond Hill, NY
Rose, Daniel, 9, 60th Street School, Niagara Falls, NY
Rose, Natalie, 10, Denison Elem., Denison, IA
Runge, Kurt, 6, St. Mary's School, Edwards, IL
Russell, James, 9, Foley Elem., Foley, AL
Ryan, Amanda, 8, Grand Isle Elem., Grand Isle, VT
Schaeffer, Priscilla, 9, Lynn Kirk Elem., Youngstown, OH
Schrier, Juanette, 8, Carlisle Elem., Carlisle, IA
Sheffield, Rachel, 8, Albany School, Albany, WI
Sherlock, Dane, 7, St. Mary's School, Edwards, IL
Slattery, Josh Rocko, 11, Bondurant Middle, Frankfort, KY
Slavin, Paul, 9, Churubusco Elem., Churubusco, IN
Smith, Carol Lee, 10, Goose Rock Elem., Manchester, KY
Snellgrove, Sherie, 9, Graceville Elem., Graceville, FL
Sousa, Matthew, 9, Greystone Elem., No. Providence, RI

Springer, William, 8, Yale Elem., Aurora, CO
St. Jean, Jason, 11, St. Thomas School, Sanford, ME
Stalvey, Jennifer, 9, Kelly Smith School, Palatka, FL
Stenson, Eve, 7, Noble Elem., Cleveland Heights, OH
Stoeckle, John, 9, Unionville Elem., Unionville, MI
Stoffer, Giniffer, 7, Piedmont Elem., Dandridge, TN
Stone, Penny, 11, Kramer Middle, Willimantic, CT
Story, Larry, Grade 4, New Gladstone School, Kansas City, MO
Suleiman, Lona, 9, Lynn Kirk Elem., Youngstown, OH
Sumcad, Jennifer, 10, Liberty School, Orland Park, IL
Sutherland, Sean, 10, Annaville Elem., Corpus Christi, TX
Taylor, Brennan, 9, Lenox School, Portland, OR
Taylor, Christina, 7, Kitty Stone Elem., Jacksonville, AL
Taylor, Jess, 8, Ohio County Elem. Middle, Rising Sun, IN
Taylor, Shayla Maria Inez, 7, Fort Crook Elem., Omaha, NE
Thiry, Brian, 7, Dag Hammarskjold School, Parma, OH
Thomas, Brent, 6, Travis School, El Paso, TX
Thomas, Derek, 11, Western Branch Elem., Chesapeake, VA
Thomas, Jennifer, 8, Park School, Munhall, PA
Thomas, Lydell, 9, Hilltop Christian School, Window Rock, AZ
Till, Tara, 10, Busansky School, Pemberton, NJ
Toppin, Nisnaka, 10, Busansky School, Pemberton, NJ
Trask, Jason, 7, Gen. John J. Stefanik School, Chicopee, MA
Tucker, John, 8, New Prospect Elem., Inman, SC
Turgeon, Michelle, 12, St. Thomas School, Sanford, ME
Turner, Heather, 8, Fairview Elem., Mora, MN
Uker, Erin, 11, Lincoln Elem., Osage, IA
Van Dyke, Robyn, 10, Hueytown Elem., Hueytown, AL
Vandiver, Aaron, 10, Westminster Christian School, Gainesville, GA
Vislocky, Nancy, 9, St. Clare School, Staten Island, NY
Vosbeck, Dana, 10, Sleepy Eye Public School, Sleepy Eye, MN
Wagner, Joey, 8, St. Catherine of Siena School, Pittsburgh, PA
Wallenstein, Angela, 10, McKinley School, Huron, SD
Walsh, Erin, 7, Oakland Grade School, Antioch, IL
Wasil, Erica, 9, St. Francis Xavier School, Cresson, PA
Watkins, Mike, 8, Timothy Ball Elem., Crown Point, IN
Webb, Jason, 8, Central Elem., Corning, AR
Webb, Jennifer, 9, Carlisle Elem., Carlisle, IA
Webster, Kate, 8, St. John of the Cross School, Western Springs, IL
Wells, Ashley, 7, Madisonville Elem., Madisonville, TX
Wiemiller, Brandon, 9, Manchester G.A.T.E., Fresno, CA
Willey, Jennifer, 8, Marcus Whitman Cowiche Elem., Cowiche, WA
Williams, Tawnya, Grade 4, Southwestern Elem., Shelbyville, IN
Wittkopp, Shannon, 7, Millbridge School, Delran, NJ
Wolfe, Hank, 9, Boonsboro Elem., Boonsboro, MD
Wolfe, Ryan, 9, Balboa Street Magnet School, Northridge, CA
Wood, Jennifer, 11, Eastgate Middle, Kansas City, MO
Yi, Min Chu, 9, Westgate Elem., Omaha, NE
Zack, Cristie, 11, St. Michael School, Chicago, IL
Zimmerman, Jenny, 6, Juda School, Juda, WI
Zimmerman, Rodney, 11, Ranchwood Elem., Yukon, OK
Zito, Michael, 9, St. Francis Cabrini School, Brooklyn, NY
Zysman, Danny, 9, Hillel School, Rochester, NY